Fountain of Inspiration

Jacqueline Sanchez

Dedication

To simply say, "I love you," is just not enough.

There aren't enough words for me to express how special you truly are…

Thank you for inspiring me in such a way that led me finally take this leap of faith to embark on this dream of mine. To see you succeed, grow and thrive is beyond encouraging. It fuels me to never give up when life gets hard. It fills me with the hope that better things are yet to come. You give me the strength to continue and the courage to not give in to my fears. Your character and strength speak the truth of who you really are. When I count my blessings I count you twice.

You inspire me to be the best version of myself.

With all my love always,

Jacqueline Sanchez

Acknowledgment

Be Bold! Follow your heart and never give up on your dreams. If you close yourself off from new endeavors, you will never know where the road may lead. I invite you to explore life with love, encouragement, passion, heartache and healing all at once. We face so many challenges in our everyday life that it is so easy to get discouraged and feel like you have failed and aren't worthy, but don't ever let those challenges take away from your purpose. Only you can make things happen if you genuinely want them to. We can sometimes experience a conglomeration of things that feels like a cosmic explosion inside.

Whether it's for a joyous reason that fills us in such a way that we cannot contain it, or it could sometimes come in the form of heartache. To carry that sense of loss through love that at times is overwhelming and feels unbearable. That is what makes us who we are. To be able to distinguish between the hurt, letting go, acceptance, and the love that we all harbor and nurture within to help us overcome, grow and find self-worth and self-love.

I've been on a journey of all these things, sometimes all at once. Writing has enabled me to let go and get through some rough patches but has also allowed me the privilege and gift of expressing my love to others.

Thank you for joining me on this journey!

About the Author

I was born on the Island of Puerto Rico and migrated to New York at about the age of 6. I am the third eldest of 6 siblings

I am very blessed to have a large family.

I have lived in the suburbs of NYC since we moved here, but I occasionally travel to my homeland. I love being outdoors. I'm not a big fan of the cold, but I enjoy the occasional snowfall and changing leaves during the fall.

I am a hopeless romantic, so writing has always been more of a personal hobby. While others have their own talents and gifts, I feel so blessed to be able to show my love for others through writing.   I began to develop my love for writing at a young age but really began to embrace my poetry writing from about the age of 12 while in Junior High..

I continued to write in my adolescence and into adulthood. While I have kept most of my writing private, some of my other pieces were published through contest entries.

Being able to write this book has not only allowed me to open a window of self-growth and opportunity, but it also enabled me to open the door and invite others into my world.

CONTENTS

Page Left Blank Intentionally

Infinite Fountain

My river has run dry

Quench my thirst, lest I die

Come quench my thirst with waters that

Flow from your infinite fountain

And take me to the peak of the highest mountains

As I slowly rise, may the birds sing me a symphony that

Calms all the restlessness I hold

As trees shed an array of colorful leaves in the coolness of

fall

That gets deposited into an empty well at the end of an

almost

Nonexistent waterfall

I diminish in my nakedness, down to the bare minerals, and

The last bit of the reserve, unsheltered as is that very same

harmonious bird

When its nest has become exposed to the elements and its'

safe haven has been revoked

Because the trees are barren, shaken, disturbed, and

provoked

Drench me with every last ounce, to the very last drop of

your water

That heals and cleanses all that needs to be removed and
leaves only what truly matters
Come water the soil that lays at the bottom of my stream
That the pebbles may be gently scattered along the ravine
That the water that flows from your infinite fountain is so
rich it thrives
With the abundance and so much life
Let's plant new seeds deep in the fertile soil so profound
That the water from your infinite fountain be completely
absorbed into the ground
So that the roots grow strong and firm yet entangled
together
That we may reap the harvest now, tomorrow, and forever
My river has run dry
Quench my thirst, lest I die.

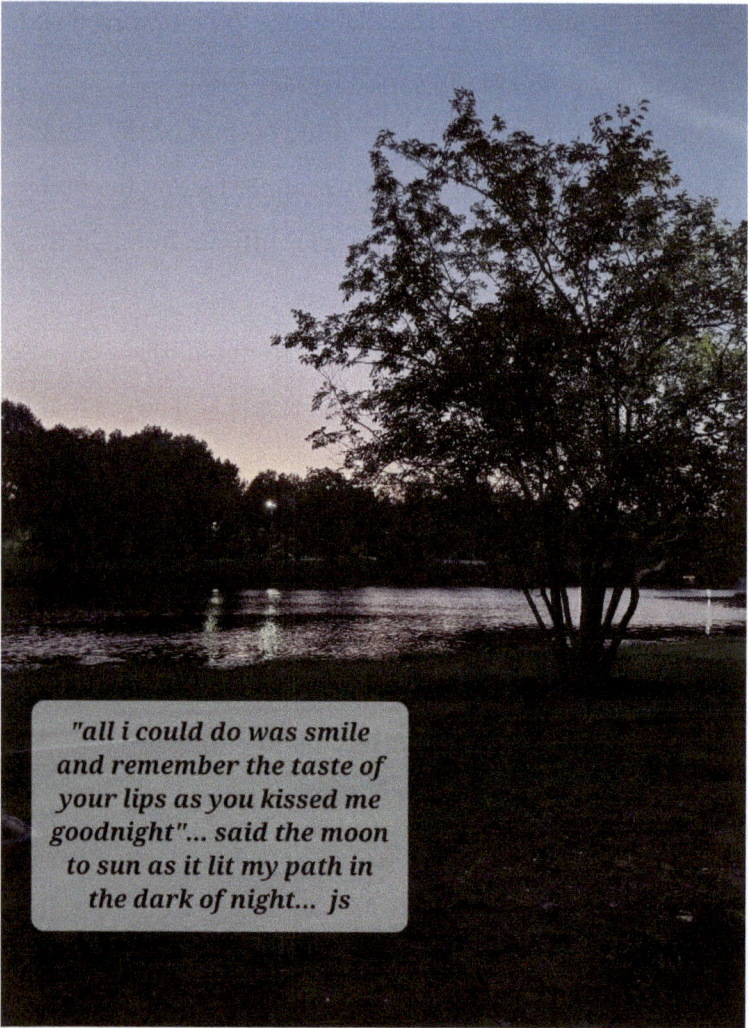

"all i could do was smile
and remember the taste of
your lips as you kissed me
goodnight"... said the moon
to sun as it lit my path in
the dark of night... js

Reflection

I saw the reflection of your soul on the still waters of the
pond
As the sun went down
And I reached out my arms to hold you, but you couldn't
be found
You were deep in your thoughts, so profound
And the pond was on fire with what was left of the sun
While the moon was dancing among stars and the Earth
slowly spun
Your heart was heavy as you carried the weight of the
world,
I felt your sadness and burdens, and I felt so small
Felt ever so helpless, for there was nothing that I could do
to ease your pain
To hold your hands and shelter you from the rain
In your reflection, I could also see your calm in the
restlessness and courage in your veins
In the days that were so long and the nights that were hard,
you feel so enslaved
I can see and feel your strength even though sometimes
your vulnerability escapes

There are moments that you go without while needing

And there are moments when you just need your space

At times the ripples in the water distort your reflection, and

it

Slowly begins to fade

Many times, you question the choices that you've made

Where the doubt resurfaces, and you become enraged

But you collect yourself and regroup again

You grow as you search for ways to be better than

yesterday

To accept things that you cannot change

Your reflection shows how full of purpose you are

And so you continue the course of your path

You are resilient and wise even in the midst of things

We fail to comprehend that we just cannot grasp

And when you are still in the silence, and you stand alone

I can still see the reflection of the most beautiful you that

you have become.

Easier

It is easier to always listen to my heart than it is to listen to

my mind

Not to give into the fear of losing you but instead to love

you

endlessly even though you aren't mine

It is so easy to get distracted to hold back the hands of the

clock and lose track

of time

It is easier to always see the best in you and overlook your

flaws

Than to turn and walk away when your silence speaks

louder than your thoughts

To see the you that no one else ever saw

It is easier to want to heal your hurt even though I am still

raw

It is easier to breathe when you are by my side

To look at the beautiful smile that you have that makes my

heart stop

But it also makes me feel alive

It is easier to forgive and to forget

Than to let you go and become strangers as if we had never

met

Sometimes it is just easier to love you more than to love

myself instead.

Heavenly Rest

Your lips burn my flesh like the fierce and sweltering
inferno of hell
Enraged as is a waterfall cascading into an infinite well
And the slivering touch of your tongue flows like spewing
lava invading every strand, every cell
Where the dam can't hold the turbulent waters
Thus, rupturing and releasing with collateral damage,
where nothing matters
Your hands roam the thriving fields that carry a scent of
freshly blooming exotic flowers
That gently rests upon the rising mountains
The look in your eyes pierces my soul
Like the deadly venomous sting of a scorpion that
scavenges in the desert
And I quiver with an agonizing pleasure full moan
Unlike the prairie, the valley is mysterious and alluring way
down below
With no fear at all, you will never get lost; you know where
to go
Your fangs puncture my veins, and with just cause, I lose
all of my senses

With my razor-sharp talons, I tattoo your back, trying to
hold on, but I am helpless
My lungs collapse, and I feel faint, completely breathless
Unhinged as I transport through each of the realms, Earth,
Wind, Water, and Fire, with an undying desire
Like a tornado and an earthquake colliding, repositioning
all of the elements
That gravity keeps together, but that disrupts the patterns of
the unpredictable weather
The shaking of the ground beneath my feet
A magnetic pull that is stronger than anything I've ever
seen.
My legs shake, and they tremble, and I whimper, and I cry
From the wrenching intensity that you see in my eyes
You thrust, and you thrust with all of your force
And you slowly seep out of your pores
Till you finally reach heaven and ask the gatekeeper to
open the door
Then you come spiraling back down to where I am and
ever so gently lay your head on my chest
Where you always find your peace and catch your breath,
Where you can always find heavenly rest...

All I Want

All I want is to fall apart peacefully; it's so hard to keep it
all together
To let you go, and with a blade, the tides we had, cut away,
to move on,
to finally sever
To detach and disconnect
To renew my balance and reset
My heart just needs to rest
I hold back the tears from these saddened eyes
That saw in you so much hope, but now burn from the hurt
they hide inside
That breach tore so much more than just the trust
That deeply came between the two of us
You built a wall too high to climb
And I failed to reach you time after time
All I want is to release the tension and this bitter anguish
There is nothing left here for us to salvage
I gather all the pieces that you left behind
From the wreckage inhabiting my bewildered mind
Can't make sense of what took place
As you stood there with a blank look on your face

All I want is to detoxify
To mend this broken heart of mine

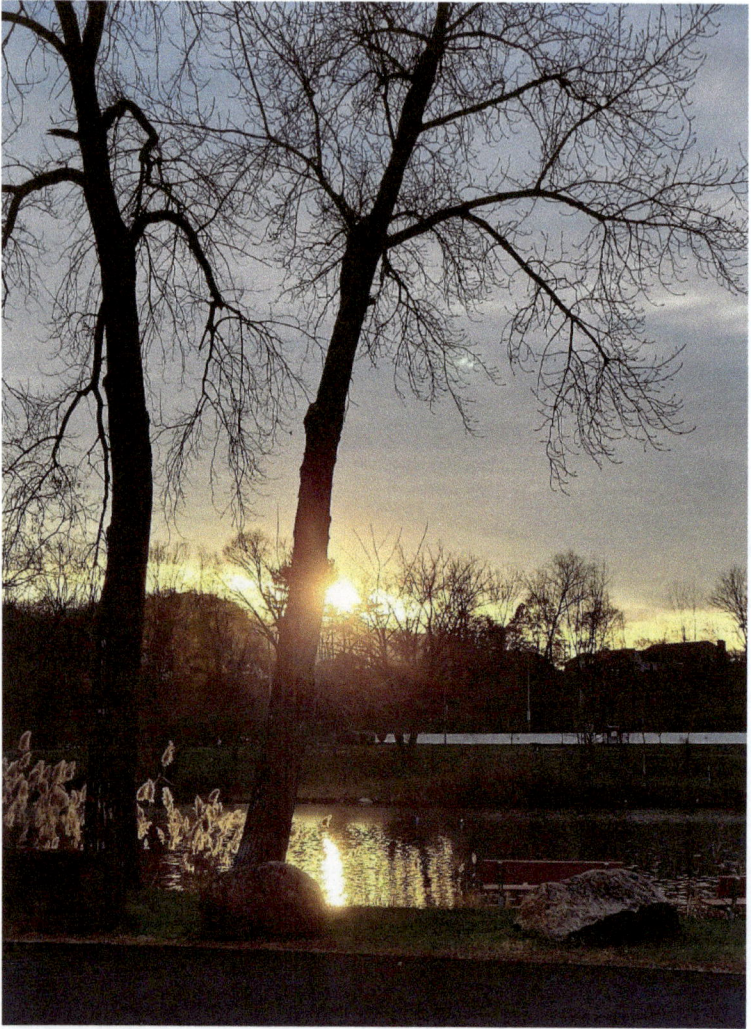

Inconsolable

Bewildered, unable to comprehend

You draw me in, then push me out again

Branded by your imprint as you make me yours once again

imprisoned in delirium, overcome with such intense

pleasure

Such agonizing pain

The taste of your lips so sweet with a bitter aftertaste

That burns like acid with every kiss you take

My knees buckle, and I give up as I gasp for air

Your tender touch dissipates, your presence no longer there

Drowning in the silence, on the brink of insanity and

despair

Cry out only to hear the echo of a voice that was once was

there

Tormented and bruised as I try to hide the scars that I wear

I can't keep count, and I lost track of the tally

Often, the weight of my world is just too heavy to carry

Inconsolable with nowhere to turn

Caught in a rainstorm of brimstone that crackles and burns

Consumed by an uncontainable blaze that spares none

To lose it all, even that which has not begun…

Chaos

And when we meet again, it will surely be like the clash of
the titans
There will be a war that will break apart the peaks of the
mountains
And make the waters rise to disrupt the flow of the streams
and the rivers
That will rattle the ground with a great moan and quiver
Lighting will strike and singe our flesh
And as the thunder roars, we will merge and fuse without
rest
We will shield one another and forget about the rest
And when we meet again, volcanos will spew their lava
with such
Rage that it consumes everything in its path
Leaving nothing but chaos in the aftermath.
And the oceans will part ways and collide again
That will provoke tsunami-like waves and torrential rain
And the rains will be like meteor showers with invisible
flames
That will engulf it all, to then let it cascade

That it may overflow into the beautiful chaos that we have made.

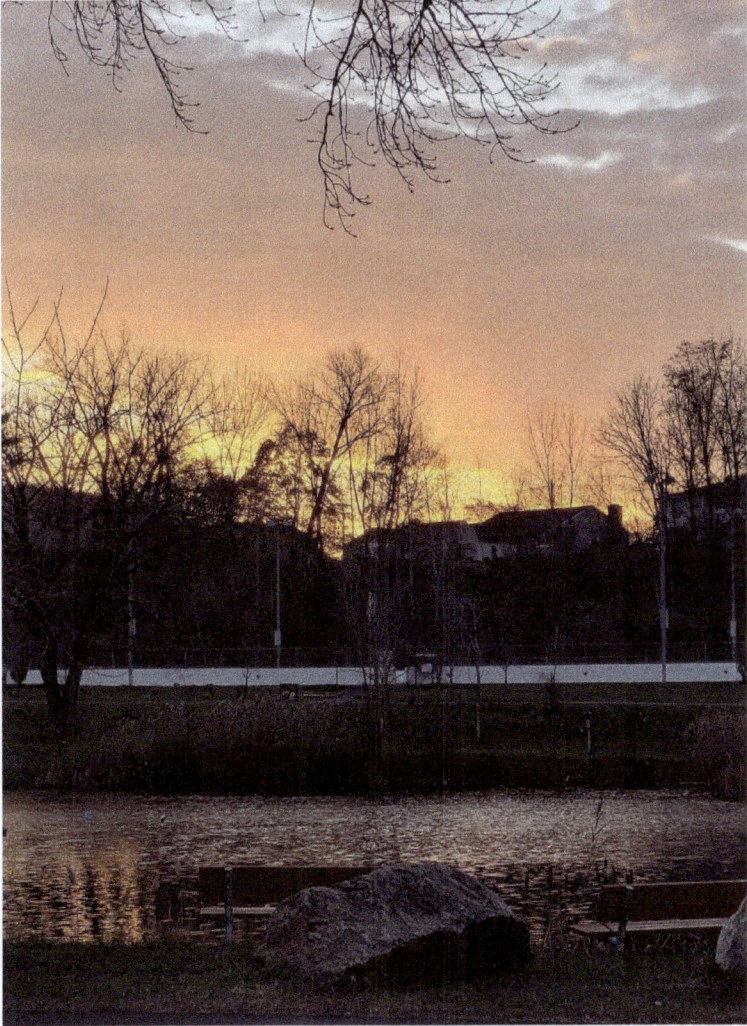

More Than Enough

The days seem eternal

The shift in the realm has gone nocturnal

The eclipse of the sun frozen in the stanza of perpetual

with the moon's hollow crevices that only echo

The space is so vast, with millions of stars

With showering meteors that leave them as mere shards

Mostly debris and full scars

The rivers run dry with a drought like no other

Pershing from the lack of springs of flowing waters

So many galaxies so apart from each other

Where once its inhabitants made it an oasis that was so

sought after…

The stars no longer burn with a fierce luster

Becoming more dull as you move closer

The oxygen depleting, vanishing, evaporating as the

The winds seize from blowing gently

Numb, No more feeling for the good and the plenty

With nowhere to run to and nowhere to hide

No cavalry; you battle alone; no one at your sides

To be humbled in such ways to shed all your pride

No longer the need to vail who you are inside

To know you've always been more than enough

Even for those that broke your trust

Even when they leave you more broken, deteriorating,

worn, falling apart,

With your inner core so full of rust

Empty, wounded, and heartless as they leave you dying

inside without ever knowing

What it is to truly love...

Nakedness

I want to see all of your nakedness

Not in the way that you shed the garments that cover your

flesh

But the rawness and grit from the battle wounds that once

profusely bled

With all of the flaws that you carry that you would much

rather forget about instead

And the fears and uncertainties that keep you awake as you

lay in your bed

The nakedness that you carry on your back feels like the

weight of the world

The same nakedness that leaves you feeling unsheltered

and out in the bitter cold

That nakedness that no one sees as you cry in the corner

when you're alone

That is always there to greet you whenever you get home…

To the emptiness that, at times, swallows you whole

I want you to see your nakedness through my eyes

To understand all of the reasons, all of the whys

For you to know that I won't pull away when you turn your

face and can't look me in the eyes

Because you're too afraid to show the real you that I know
you hide inside
The transparency of your nakedness that makes up every
strand of you, and you alone
That nakedness that I want to tend to and nurture, that has
the purest of all the souls that I have ever known.

No Words At All

Broken with the heart's inability to heal the hurt

Because the mind can reason, but the heart won't

Endless tears like a waterfall they flow

To release and cleanse the soul

Can't sleep as thoughts of you flood my mind

To be here without you by my side

The insomnia finally sets in

I am feeling empty with the solitude it brings

Can't grasp the idea that you are so far away

Wishing you were here in my arms, that you would have

stayed

So unavailable and so far out of reach

Slowly drifting further away from the safety of the beach

Left wondering where I went so wrong

Feeling so out of place, like I don't belong

So vulnerable without your shield to protect me from the

raging storm,

To fall for you was so natural and so quick, but to forget

you, will take me so long

The freshly sharpened blade of your indifference cuts so

deep

And the invisible blood that no one can sees gushes and
seeps
Until there is nothing left of me
My heart, in an eternal dormant state of sleep
Numb, to never again feel what you made me feel
Knowing that this is where it ends feels so surreal
How to remove the spike full dagger that punctured my
heart
That rips my insides to shreds, and I should have known
from the start
To say goodbye with no words at all
Feeling hollow and so very small
Frozen to the core as the cruelty of winter sets into place
Lost through the labyrinth of time and space
Covered in the blanket of snow left from the blizzard of
your harsh goodbye
And as the wind spews jagged shards of ice
The brutal winds howl as the warmth of the sun subsides...
Ashes are all that remains from the fierce fire that once
burned
To capture the lesson in what was to be learned
With time you will be but a faint and distant part of my
history

That will have been deposited deep down in the bank of my memory…

Time

I feel the utter sting

As you walk away and as all my walls come caving in

I am swallowed by the echoing silence that is unseen and

unheard

Drenched by the emptiness and the hurt

To love is to give one's self until you're completely

consumed by the burn

Of knowing you will not be back tomorrow

To grieve in the unforgiving sorrow

No more sun to fill my days

Just the raindrops to fill in the puddles along the way

To search for you among the crowd

To wear a smile and hide the frown

To yearn for your sweet caress

I will miss you more than words can ever express

No one can or will ever understand the life that you brought

to me

That is now being stripped away as I set you free

I can never lose what was never mine

I can only thank you for the

The most precious gift that you could've ever given me

Your time...

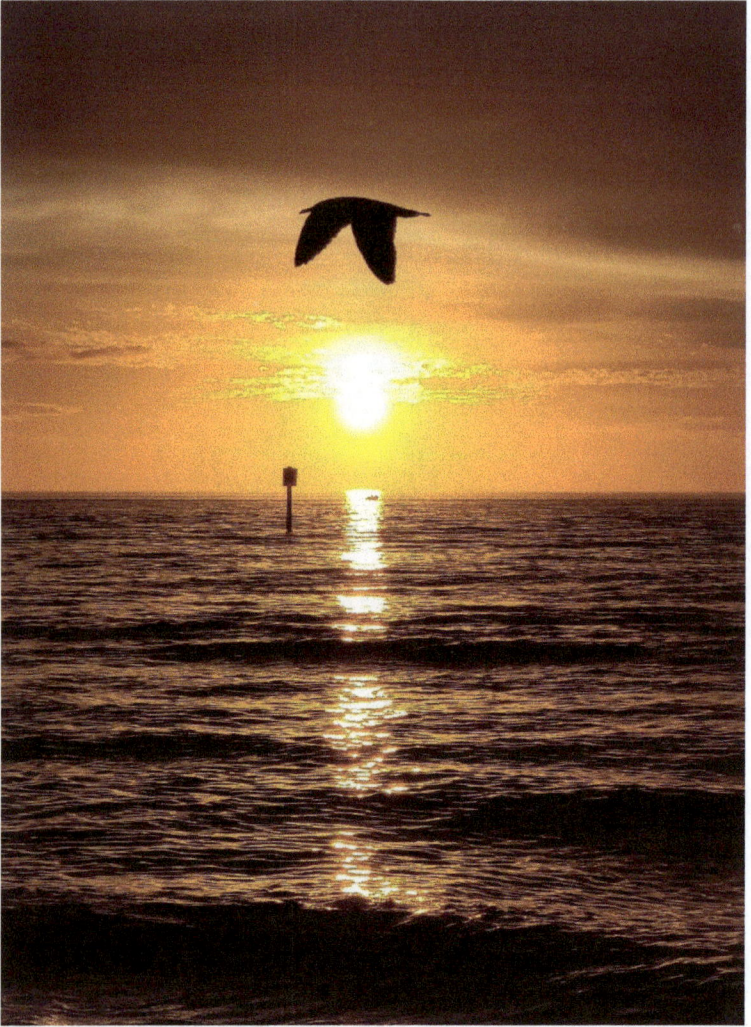

Teach Me

You taught me to laugh even when I was without reason

You taught me to let go of all of the things that hurt

That it's all temporary, as are the seasons

You taught me that tears are essential for healing and

cleansing the soul

And not just for me, but for all

You taught me how to take slow deep breaths to inhale the

fresh air

And to take in the aroma of the flowers dancing in the

breeze without a care

You taught me to see with my heart and not with my eyes

And that even though my wings were a little bit broken, I

could still fly

You taught me love through the language of touch

With your sweet caresses and tender kisses that always

meant so much

You taught me humbleness with your soft-spoken heart

As you collected all of my broken parts

You taught me patience in all of the times you made me

wait

And you taught me strength through your kindness

And taught me that we truly embrace life through the
lessons from our mistakes
You taught me to listen and not just hear
As I poured myself into your ears
You'd nurture my anxiousness and teach me to be calm
When in my times of grief, you'd hold me in your arms
You taught me to give all that I am, to love without
regret—
But now you need to teach me how to erase all the
memories, that linger in your absence, as I live with this
pain,
Teach me to forget…

Innocence

When I look into his eyes, I see the innocence of a boy

Standing before me, so tall, so proud, and so poised

With a smile that casts out the sun like an eclipse

And brightens the universe with a mere glimpse

With a pure heart that speaks only truth

That listens, heals, soothes, and judges not,

With open arms to hold me close and tight

To hear his heartbeat through the night

When I feel the touch of his hands

I feel the strength of a courageous man

And when I hear the sound of his voice, my knees tremble

to resist his call, I am too weak, I am not able

To inhale the scent of his skin

To be completely soaked with all of him

Submerged—

Rescue me as I drown in his lagoon

My feet are planted on the ground, yet I can still reach the

moon,

A kiss from his soft lips to stop the Earth from rotating on

its axis

To graze upon his thriving green and lush pastures

To indulge in all the fruits that he bears

To feel his warm and sweet caress when he's no longer

there

Trapped in his enigma, lost without a compass, nowhere

bound

Too deep and too far gone to be found

To be filled with an absolutely infinite and everlasting joy

From a man that still holds true to the innocence of a boy...

Dream Awake

Sweet kisses in the rain

To feel your tender embrace once again

Wrap your arms around me like a shield

To get lost and find each other in a sunflower field

To gaze into each other's eyes

In a daydream, being whisked away as time passes by

Sipping hot cocoa by the fire

To talk endlessly through the night, even when we're tired

A smile as bright as a shooting star

To feel you close even when we are far apart

To hear you whisper in my ear,

For you to calm and ease all of my fears

To see the sunrise kiss the night sky away

To be showered with the sun's warmth of its tender rays

To wash the sand from our feet with the gentle soothing

waves

Even when you are beside me, you are still too far away

Because loving you... is to always dream awake...

Essence of My Being

Beautiful as the sunset in the west and the sunrise in the
east
Gentle and refreshing like a cool summer breeze
A smile that radiates parallel to the horizon which puts my
heart at ease
The calming whispers of your voice that soothe my aching
soul
Soft and delicate like the petals of a blooming rose
A kiss so intense that it takes my breath away
So drawn to you, in a brief instant, I am swept away
Your sweet, tender embrace takes me to that very place
Where I get lost in the vast oceans of your eyes
Captivated, imprisoned, mesmerized
I find myself drowning, overwhelmed by the storm that
rages
in the depths within you
That very storm that grows and thrives within me too
To give myself with no regard, or fear of losing track
To close my eyes and see you gazing back
Where your stare pierces the very essence of my being

Surpassing all my senses

Breaking down my walls, my defenses,

To slowly bring me back as you take me by the hand

While time erases our footprints in the sand…

44

I Want to Make Love

I want to make love…

The kind of love that says good morning and good night

That calls in the middle of your hectic day just to say,

"Hello, I am thinking about you."

To build on the memories that we carry

For the rest of our days

The kind of love that isn't afraid to be vulnerable and

knows how to say,

"I am sorry" and mean it

That gives without hesitation

That kind of love that will always kisses your forehead just

because

They wrap you in their arms and never want to let you go,

and it feels like home

That is soft-spoken yet firm in truth and is understanding

That knows how to forgive and truly is unconditional

The kind of love that is pure and transparent in all of its

ways

I want to make love…

That kind that watches sunsets with you,

Then counts the stars that accompany the moon

That makes you smile when you're feeling down

The kind of love that holds your hand in the dark so that

you know that you're not alone

The kind of love that says it all without words but with just

the look in their eyes

The sweetest kind of love that's so intense it leaves an

imprint, and you never feel their absence

The kind of love that warms the soul

And fills your heart I want to make love…

Not to you, but with you…

Metamorphosis

Cocooning, transitioning, closed off, unavailable

Growing, morphing, and reaching for the unobtainable

Wings restricted by the lack of space and time

So raw, textured, and so unrefined:

Exposed to the explosions of all the elements in this

abstract containment that I

am in

Capsuled and submerged in the goo and acid that break

down all the toxins

That anchors me down in the process of this transformation

That will one day lead me down the path of my ultimate

purpose, my salvation

With each passing moment, I evolve a little more

Without knowing what is to come, what's in store

The days are long without you, but much longer are the

nights

That come with grief and darkness since the moon

withdraws her light

And holds back the rebellious stars in the sky

I battle and struggle to hold on tight

And even when nothing is going right

I know my wings are almost ready to take flight

To set out on new endeavors with delight

As I walk across this tightrope we call life

As my own kind of butterfly

Need For More

Wicked eyes intense like the sun

Scorches the flesh with a flameless fire that burns

Allured and captivated, like a moth to a flame

I am trapped in your enchantment, a pawn in your game

Hair dark and mysterious like the evening sky

With a smile brighter than a starry night

Hands so gentle and so strong,

A sweet caress that awakens a raging storm

Lips so soothing and sweet as honeydew,

To quench my thirst only like you do

A kiss breathtaking, agonizing, relentless

like the waves that crash onto the shore

To lose myself every time in undying desire

That leaves me with the need for more…

Armageddon

Time stood still, and the Earth would violently shake
beneath our feet

And volcanoes would erupt their lava and scorch us with
such sweltering heat

Burning our flesh like the surface of the sun

As if an Armageddon had begun

And a whirlwind romance took flight that led us astray

Where we'd come to meet in our secret place

Where the world did not exist

And transparency just was, with intense utter bliss

Completely vulnerable in each other's arms

Where our souls would collide like the shooting stars

With two heartbeats that would fuse together and beat as
one

Where our minds and hearts could freely roam

Where to be in your presence always felt like home

With lighting in our hands, our palms would come together

And in a moment, just as thunder roars,

We could feel the meaning of forever

Where our lips would hinge one to the other

And it rained the sweetest of kisses, and the love was endless

And we were infinite, eternal and restless —

Entirely consumed by the brimstone and fire of that

Armageddon

Where we'd perish, but the flame would burn forever…

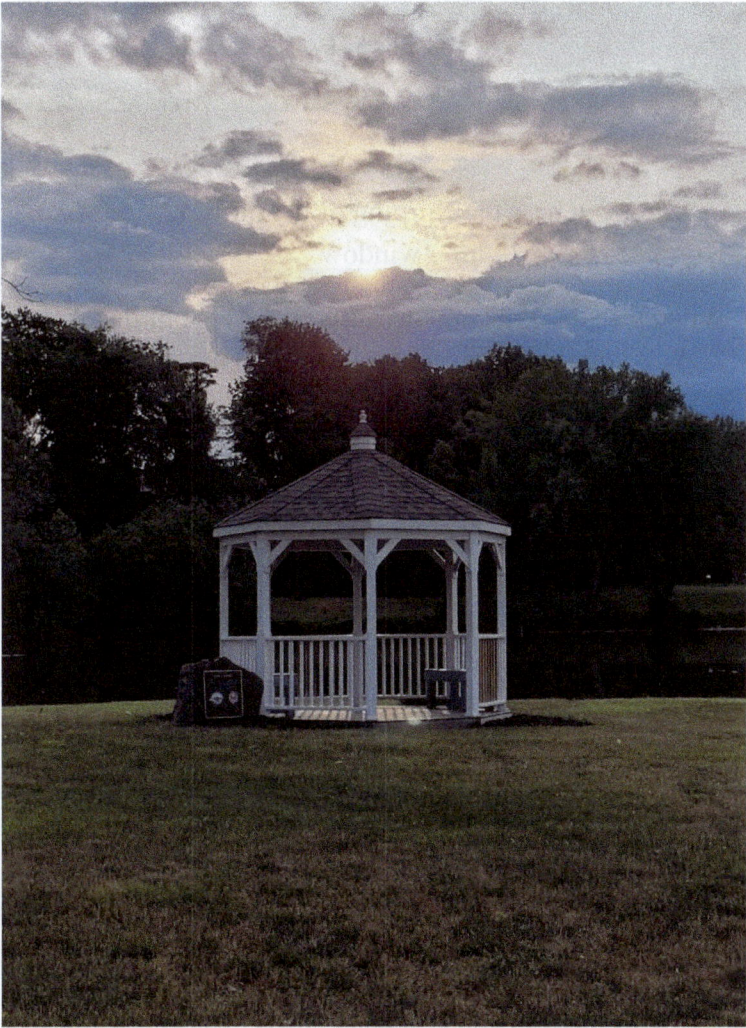

When...

When you hear the chirping of the birds outside your
window

When the sun rises, it is because I asked the birds to wish
you the sweetest of all the good mornings

And when you hear the owls hooting in the evening
underneath the moonlight

It is because I asked the owls to wish you the most peaceful
and restful of nights

And when you feel the warmth of the sun on your lips
throughout your day, it is because I asked the sun to give
you all of my kisses

When you feel the gentle breeze blowing your hair as you
walk along the shore

It is because I asked the wind to caress you on my behalf

And when you hear the waves crashing on the sand,

May you hear my voice in

the distance saying all of the "I love you's" that were never
said...

When you walk through the garden and fields and smell the
sweet aroma of

all the freshly blooming flowers

May you remember the scent of my skin

As I wrapped my arms around you…

And should you ever feel the raindrops fall upon your eyes,
it is because

I asked the clouds in the sky to show you how much my
heart is missing you…

A Touch of His Lips

A man kissed me once, took my breath away, and I
instantly fell

Entangled in the web of his enchantment, just can't break
the spell

The lingering aroma of his scent still permeates the walls of
my inner being

Left here without his touch in a state of mourning, still
grieving

To live out my deepest and most intimate fantasies like
with no one else

Living and breathing, but losing myself—

Ignited a blaze, way down in my core that burns with a fury
of vengeance

Intense like the surface of the sun, ravenous and relentless

An inferno that consumes me all at once with no way to put
out the flame

Never again will I be the same.

A man kissed me once and opened the floodgates of hell

And I drank the poisonous water that over flowed from his
well

Completely parched from the sand storm, I dove right in, completely drenched

Stumbling over myself from the drunkenness, and it was so that my thirst was quenched

Very quickly, the effects of the poison set in

Feeling feverish, fatigued and faint, my heart races from the adrenalin

The blood in veins flows like lava but corrodes just like acid

For a mere moment pausing the beat of my heart and no one else but only he can restart it

A man kissed me once and took me as high as the stars in the constellation

There I was, floating on the surface of his fierce yet tranquil oceans

Like a tornado, abruptly, he plucked me right out of the ground

And dispersed all of my pieces, not to be found

I spun in the chaos of his heart in the torturous funnel

In utter darkness with no hope or light at the end of the tunnel

Every day that goes by without his touch, I breathe a little less

And diminish a little more

How to erase all of his kisses when all my heart wants is more?

All three of these men are all one in the same

With just a touch of his lips, I surrender again and again…

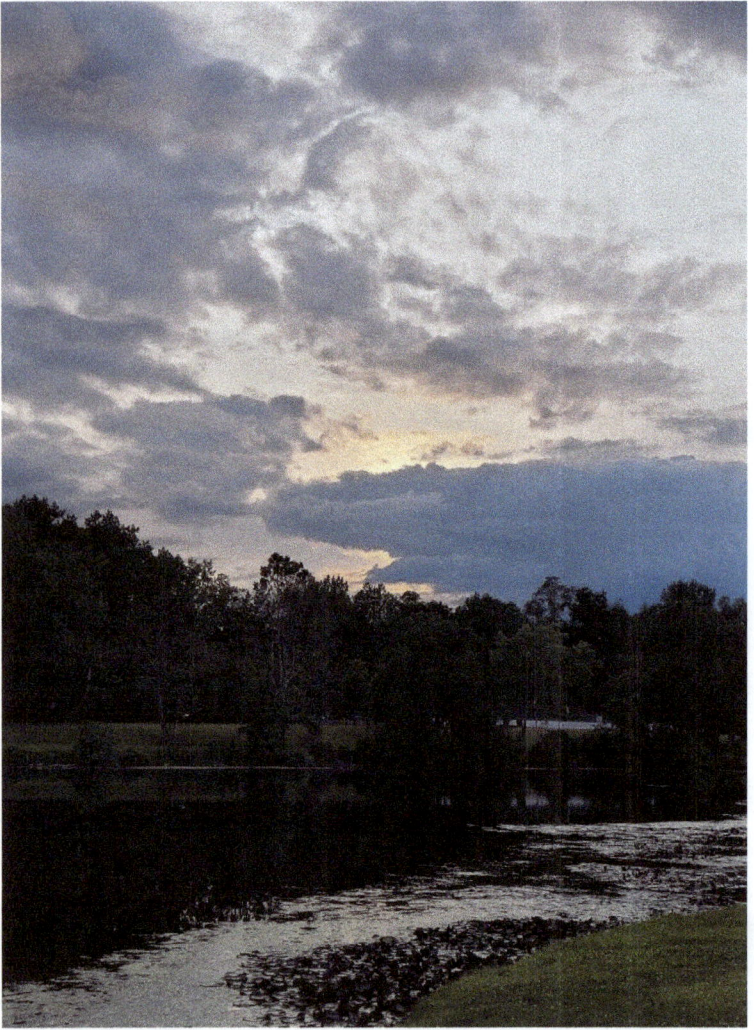

Cotton Candy Sunset

I will never look at the sunset in the same way ever again

Because I will never be able to tame the desires that my
heart craves

To caress your face and hold your hand

To catch your radiant smile in a glance

The evening lurks, and the day draws to a close

It is then that I miss you most

The cotton candy sunset gently kisses the night sky

Sprinkled with pixie dust that falls from the shooting stars

And I quickly make a wish and close my eyes

To always walk with you by my side

With the spoonful of orange creamsicle ice cream and
blueberry snow cones

With the taste of a fruit medley that I savor in silence but
never alone

Like the sweetness of honeydew melon that gushed from
your lips with every

Kiss that you gave, all of the lingering memories that
together we have made

And while the moon tucked in the sun with the aroma of
honey-roasted almonds in the air

I will never forget that,

With every cotton candy sunset, no matter where I am and
how far you are,

I know that I will always find you there…

Just Like That...

And just like that I fell…

With his humble gentle way

With his kisses that took my breath away

That no other man can ever erase

With the touch of his sweet embrace

The imprint that he left without a trace

To be in his arms, in my favorite place.

The way he would run his fingers through my hair

All the tender moments that we shared

That kept me going when he wasn't there

The strong and stern tone in the way he speaks

The look in his eyes would get me weak in the knees

And just like that, I close my eyes…

And I remember, relive and reminisce

The taste of honey flowing from his soft and luscious lips

And just for an instant, I am wrapped in the warmth of his
arms that shelter my soul

And I give him everything I am, give him my all

But then, just like that…

The clouds fill the sky and the rain sets in

My mind and heart are left to wonder how and where you've been.

The story of us, two doves with broken wings that cannot fly

Who, just like that, became strangers once again in the middle of the night...

And Hello Again...

And hello again…

I hope with all of me that this finds you well and for you to know that you are

Always being thought of…

What I wouldn't give to see that beautiful smile of yours

And whisper in your ear just how much I adore you even more so than before

For you to feel my warm embrace

For you to know this will always be your home,

That here, you will always have a place

For you to hear and feel my heart racing from inside my chest

Where you are loved the most when you're at your worst,

And even more than when you're at your best

That when the day is long and hard you can lay your head upon my chest to rest

And that all of the kisses I've withheld would shower and cascade over every ounce of you

So that you may feel refreshed and renewed

For you to know that what I feel for you is with the purest
of intentions and so full of truth

For you to see how even when all the words always fall
short of what my heart tries to convey

that my love grows for you more and more with every
passing day…

Even More So...

I will never tell you how much I miss you, but I hope you're doing well.

That all of the pieces of your puzzle have been found and that you are finally all put

together

Like a work of art with a marvelous story to tell.

Seamless, without the rough edges or tears, because you've been remastered and

repaired

That the outline of your silhouette is smooth and rich like a warm cup of coco on a

cold brisk day.

to remind you that I still love you, even more so with every passing day

That I haven't forgotten you in any way

That it still hurts when I hear your name and

That my life without you in it hasn't been the same

all I ever wanted was for you to be more than just ok

That you could see yourself in these eyes of mine

That saw not just your outer shell but also who you are
inside

That always longed for you, even as you stood before me,
by my side

And even when you'd come and go, as does the rising tide

So I hope to see you one day from afar, and smile to see
you walking with her by

your side,

to see all the love that she holds for you with just the look
in her eyes

that as you walk your journey hand in hand, you keep her
as the most valuable

treasure

that you will ever find,

in that same way that I saw and felt, even more so than
even when it was you and I...

Silent Cry

And while I stood there in the rain, every rain drop
absorbed the tears

That fell from my eyes, and in the midst of the chaos, I
finally heard your silent cry

I heard you shout to the winds, the Earth and the sky

"I am not the one, if you'd only see that, but you don't even
try"

I heard you say, "I love your body, your touch and your
kiss,

But your mind, your heart and your soul, those things don't
matter,

Those things I don't miss…"

Despite all the flags that waved in the wind

I wasn't afraid to take the risk and let you in

I gave you all that I was, all that I had, and all that I could

And with your carnal desires, you took and you took

You push me away, then reeled back in with your hook

When you were done, you'd just rip out that page in your
book

And when you had nothing better to do

You'd begin writing anew

Knowing I'd be there right there where you left me, where I always stood

And you never had to worry about being questioned or being misunderstood

Because my love for you had always been unconditional, perhaps too good to be true

And in your silent cry, I also heard you say, "I am a little bit broken, and I don't know how to love,

I don't mean to hurt you, but right now, you're more than I can handle,

You're a bit too much."

Your silent cry was so loud, with your shouts of indifference, that mine were completely shut out

Your alter ego resurfaced, and so did the doubts

Yet there I stood, trying to heal what I didn't break, what wasn't and would never be mine

And while I never expected , I was so hopeful time after time

You'd just smile with a smile as big as the sky, and your words couldn't be heard

But I could hear them through your beautiful lying eyes…

I just had to learn to read between the lines…

Your silence spoke with such depth

As I was drowning, you left me for dead…

But I fought and fought with my last dying breath

When the last bit of air escaped from my lungs,

It caused a rippling effect

And when rings in the water were no more,
They vanished just as did the rest…

And while for you, it was a moment or two

There in my quiet place… I saw the rest of my life with
you…

Through all of my sadness and hurt I saw what was meant
to be seen

That sometimes, some of the ones that we love are just
meant to be loved only in the perimeters from within

To be carried forever deep down inside,

And even though you've healed and moved on,

Sometimes you still silently cry…

Just a Reflection...

And if you want to know how I am, where and with who
I am in a state of awe and wonder, yet still perplexed,
But in a place that brings me peace and takes me far away,
I am accompanied by solitude
The moon is hiding from me, not to see me mourning,
The sun gave me his back without a care or hesitation,
And I sit among the weeds that sway and dance as they
gather together,
Enjoying the cool evening breeze,
There's a symphony of strings playing the most beautiful
instrumental music I've ever heard...
Where the turtles come to gossip and the swans only visit
in the budding spring.
Where the frog can only hope to find his princess to be
transformed by her kiss.
Where the fountain sprouts love and abundance...
So now, you know...